MW00679596
by
Linda Rector-Page,
N.D., Ph.D.
Stress,
Depression
&
Overcoming Addictions

The Healthy Healing Library Series

ISBN:1-884334-33-4

Published by Healthy Healing Publications, Inc.
16060 Via Este,
Sonora, Ca., 95370.

Booklets in the Library Series

- Renewing Female Balance
- Do You Have Blood Sugar Blues?
- A Fighting Chance For Weight Loss & Cellulite Control
- The Energy Crunch & You
- Gland & Organ Health - Taking Care
- Heart & Circulation - Controlling Blood Cholesterol
- Body Cleansing & Detoxification to Fight Disease
- Allergy Control & Management & Overcoming Asthma
- Stress, Tension & Pain Relief
- Colds & Flu & You - Building Optimum Immunity
- Fighting Infections with Herbs - Controlling STDs
- Beautiful Skin, Hair & Nails Naturally
- Don't Let Your Food Go to Waste
- Do You Want to Have a Baby? Natural Prenatal Care
- Menopause & Osteoporosis
- Power Plants - Prime Nutrients from Herbs
- Herbal Therapy For Kids
- Renewing Male Health & Energy
- Cancer - Can Alternative Therapies Help?
- "Civilization" Diseases - CFS, Candida, Lupus & More
- Overcoming Arthritis With Natural Therapies

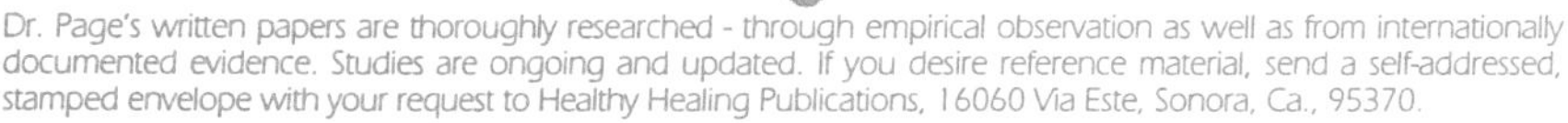

Dr. Page's written papers are thoroughly researched - through empirical observation as well as from internationally documented evidence. Studies are ongoing and updated. If you desire reference material, send a self-addressed, stamped envelope with your request to Healthy Healing Publications, 16060 Via Este, Sonora, Ca., 95370.

The Healthy Healing Library Series

As affordable health care in America becomes more difficult to finance and obtain, more attention is being focused on natural therapies and healthy preventive nutrition. Over 65% of Americans now use some form of alternative health care, from vitamins to massage therapy to herbal supplements. Everyone wants and needs more information about these methods in order to make informed choices for their own health and that of their families.

Herbal medicines are especially in the forefront of modern science today because they have the proven value of ancient wisdom and a safety record of centuries.

TABLE OF CONTENTS

❈ Stress Management — Pg. 5
  ❦De-stressing things you can do — Pg. 7

❈ Alternative Therapies For Depression — Pg. 8
  ❦Herbal Tonics — Pg. 10
  ❦Massage Therapy — Pg. 10
  ❦Guided Imagery — Pg. 11

❈ Stress Stages
  ❦Stress & Your Glands — Pg. 12
  ❦Stress & Your Heart — Pg. 13
  ❦Stress & Digestion — Pg. 14
  ❦Stress & Immune Response — Pg. 16
❈ Tension Headaches — Pg. 17
  ❦Aromatherapy for Stress — Pg. 19

❈ Stress & Addictions — Pg. 23
❈ The Nineties Addiction - Work — Pg. 25

Stress Management:
Relaxing Your Life

Stress is the universal enemy of modern mankind. Most Americans today are running harder and harder to stay in the same place. Many people seem to be under stress most of the time, depleting energy reserves, and creating over-acid systems that never allow for relaxation. We try to get as much done as we can in as short a time as possible. Sometimes we try to do as many things as possible at the same time!

Financial obligations, job pressures, seeking work in an increasingly down-sized job market, family demands, emotional problems, health concerns, and lack of rest and leisure can overwhelm even the most stable, well-adjusted nature. While facing challenges and difficulties helps us to grow and learn, (if we didn't have problems we would be dead), **prolonged, chronic stress** places tremendous demands on the body and mind. Everyone is affected by varying degrees of stress. At best, stress causes useless fatigue; at worst, it is dangerous to health.

Stress is our physical and emotional response to the demands of life. The key to health is how we respond to stress.

Other than an inherited propensity, stress is usually at the heart of heart disease. It is a major cause of headaches, hypoglycemia, arthritis, reduced immune response and some cancers. Indeed, most degenerative diseases are stress related. Stress irritates the body in the form of gastritis, ulcers and colitis. It irritates the mind in the form of moodiness, burn-out, overuse of drugs, depression and anxiety. Stress directly depletes the adrenal glands. In prolonged cases, the adrenals cannot raise blood sugar when necessary and hypoglycemia results. In severe cases, such as Addison's disease, the adrenals enlarge to the point of hemorrhaging and tissue death results. Stress affects the reproductive organs, libido and sexual ability. It leads to irritable bladder, acne, eczema, psoriasis, nervous tics, muscle spasms, high cholesterol, and even to baldness.

Emotions are also a key factor in stress. The inability to express emotion, loneliness, sadness, grief, and chronic depression can be just as damaging to health because they affect immune response.

Stressful situations probably aren't going to go away. So how can we handle them better?

The human body is designed to handle stressful situations. Since we thrive and are challenged by some of them, the goal should not be to avoid all stress, but to maintain a high degree of health and survive stress well. Poor health cannot be blamed on stress. We fall prey to stress **because** of poor health.

Controlling chronic stress often requires reorganization of lifestyle. Major problems usually require major change.

Nutrition has a major impact on how stress affects each individual. Stress depletes excessive amounts of nutrients in the body. These need to be replaced. During periods of intense stress, nutritional needs are greatly intensified. Prolonged nutritional deficiencies compound stress effects. Nutritional support is far better for dealing with stress than drugs, sedatives or chemical anti-depressants.

☛ Eliminate sugar, caffeine and processed foods for better biochemical balance.

☛ Add vegetable protein and mineral-rich foods, such as soy foods, sea foods, and sprouts to your diet.

☛ Supplement your diet with B vitamins, calcium, magnesium and potassium to nourish your nerves and minimize stress.

Herbs are wonderful medicinals for overcoming stress naturally. They are rich in replacement minerals, trace minerals, and plant enzymes. They provide inner strength with bio-active, stabilizing amino acids and electrolytes that help restore body and mind energy. They correct nutrient deficiencies with vitamin B complex, vitamin C and bioflavonoids that fortify you for inner calm when the going gets tough. Sometimes you can even expect miracles.

The most popular, effective herbal combination we know to reduce stress and tension helps by repairing damaged nerve sheathing. It is a powerful nervine that quiets and soothes the brain without the addictive side effects of valium compounds. It supports healthy nerve structure, and provides a soothing influence on the brain. It promotes stabilizing body balance during high stress times. It particularly helps control acid-produced stress and emotional anxiety. It works rapidly, often within 30 minutes. It may be taken alone, or along with other healing programs to allow the body to heal itself faster and easier. The capsule formula looks like this:

BLACK COHOSH, CULTIVATED LADY SLIPPER, SCULLCAP, KAVA KAVA, BLACK HAW, HOPS, VALERIAN RT., EUROPEAN MISTLETOE, WOOD BETONY, OATSTRAW, LOBELIA.

A relaxing tea to combat stress headaches, nerves and fatigue soothes the mind and restores mental energy. It may be taken anytime for a nice mental pick-me-up.
LEMON BALM, SPEARMINT, LICORICE, YERBA SANTA, LEMONGRASS, ROSEBUDS, CINNAMON, ROSEMARY, ORANGE PEEL, PASSION FLWR.

Environmental conditions such as chemicals and pollutants in our food, air and water also stress our bodies and add to feelings of anxiety. Minimize your exposure to pollution. I know a good job is hard to find, but if your work place is unhealthy because of pollutants, there are many things you can do, from getting your company to take healthy precautions to wearing a dust mask. Reduce the use of strong chemicals, pesticides and solvents in your home.

Proven de-stressing things you can do:

Put your life in perspective - learn not to overreact, or take things too personally. Develop a sense of humor about life's little surprises - see them as an opportunity instead of a curse. Shifting away from having "things" rule your life is a good first move.

Learn some time management techniques. Delegate more, say no when demands from others or yourself aren't realistic.

Take a short get-away vacation. Even a week-end in the beauty of nature can do wonders to change outlook, emotions and body chemistry. **You have to unwind before you can unleash.**

Take an alternating hot and cold "hydrotherapy" shower to stimulate circulation and clear your head. This is especially good at the end of a hard work day, before you go out in the evening. This is a never-fail de-stresser for me; you might be surprised at how your attitude and mood will change.

Get a massage - full or partial, self-given or by another, to stimulate oxygen uptake and blood flow.

Meditation is a massage for the mind. It takes practice, but can bring stillness to chaotic thoughts.

Get a little help from your friends. Just by listening, they can help you get through tough times. Nourish your friendships. People

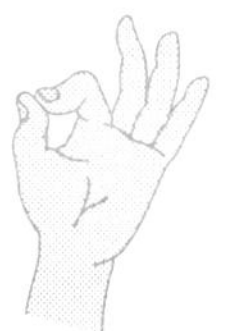

with supporting friends handle stress much better than those who rely only on themselves.

*Get some aerobic exercise and fresh air 3 to 4 days a week, to increase nutrition, tissue oxygen levels and body balance. Exercise reduces muscle tension as much as 25%, and reduces anxiety for up to 2 hours after each exercise session. Diaphragmatic breathing, (like taking a deep breath before a hard task) is especially good for mental equilibrium. Get early morning sunlight on the body every day possible.

Can alternative therapies help when there is severe emotional stress or chronic depression?

Depression can make you sick. Chronic depression is a serious, life-limiting, immune-suppressing state that disrupts the lives of **more than 30 million Americans.** Eighty percent of terminal cancer patients have a history of chronic depression. The mental and emotional state that we call depression can stem from a wide range of causes. There seem to be five broad origins for depression:
1) Great loss, as of a spouse or child, and the inability to mourn or express grief.
2) Bottled-up anger and aggression turned inward.
3) Behavior, often learned as a child, that gets desired attention or controls relationships.
4) Biochemical imbalance characterized by amino acid and other nutrient deficiencies.
5) Drug-induced depression from alcohol, sugars or prescription drugs.

When there is no apparent neurotic or psychotic basis for depression, nutrition, guided imagery and massage therapy can be far more beneficial than years of psychiatric treatment.

Severe stress weakens and imbalances the nervous system, leading to anxiety or depression. Herbal formulas can specifically help with nervous system stress support.

Herbs that have traditionally been used to lift depression include St. John's wort, rosemary, lavender, damiana and gotu kola. Herbs help restore the body's homeostasis when it is assaulted by stress. Herbal combinations are designed to address many aspects of stress symptoms.

The herbal extract below is strong enough to deal with severe symptoms, yet calming, soothing and restorative. It is one of the most effective fomulas available in relieving nerve pain and muscle constriction. It helps the adrenals respond to stress by increasing the utilization of ascorbic acid stores. It aids repair of nerve sheathing. It uses rich herbal minerals to control acid-produced stress.
BLACK COHOSH RT., SCULLCAP LF., BLACK HAW, WOOD BETONY, KAVA KAVA, CARROT EXT., HONEY.

The following herbal tea is calming and soothing to the nerves. It is particularly effective for tension head, neck and shoulder aches.
CATNIP ROSEMARY, CHAMOMILE, PEPPERMINT, BLUE VIOLET, WOOD BETONY, GOTU KOLA, FEVERFEW FLWR., WHITE WILLOW BARK, BLESSED THISTLE.

For a measure of calm during grief, anxiety, or unidentifiable lingering depression, the following formula provides tranquility for nervous tension and severe headaches. Results are noticed almost immediately and are reported to be cumulative against depression. It is particularly helpful in re-balancing and rebuilding the nervous system and restoring mental tranquility after severe stress.
SCULLCAP, LADY SLIPPER, VALERIAN RT., ROSEMARY LF., HOPS, CATNIP WOOD BETONY, PEPPERMINT, CELERY SD., CINNAMON.

Long-standing depression usually involves allergies. Eliminate foods to which you are allergic. Eliminate sugars and refined foods from your diet. Avoid foods with chemical preservatives and flavorings. Avoid addicting stimulants like caffeine, alcohol and tobacco.

☞**Add 5000mg of vitamin C to your daily diet.**

☞**Add DLPA, an amino acid that increases neurotransmitters, and acts as a mood elevating supplement without the side effects of anti-depressant drugs.**

☞**Add an essential fatty acid source, such as EVENING PRIMROSE OIL to your daily diet.**

Herbs are rich sources of calming minerals

VALERIAN/WILD LETTUCE EXTRACT includes highly absorbable sources of naturally-occurring calcium and magnesium. These herbs are synergistic as muscle relaxants for nervous tension and restful sleep. They are especially helpful for restless, hyperactive children. It may be used before retiring by both children and adults (see child dosage on page 28) to calm nerves and ease restlessness.

Calcium and magnesium are nature's primary mineral elements for calming and stabilizing the body. The following herb source mineral combination is also rich in organic silica for bone, tissue and collagen formation, and for hair and nail strength.
ELEMENTAL CALCIUM 59MG, ELEM. MAGNESIUM 31MG, ELEM. SILICON 560MCG - FROM CARROT, OATSTRAW, WATERCRESS, PAU D'ARCO, BORAGE SD., ROSEMARY, DANDELION, ALFALFA.

A hot seaweed, mineral bath is nature's perfect body/psyche balancer. Remember how good you feel after a walk in the ocean? Seaweeds purify ocean pollutants, and they can do the same for your body. Rejuvenating effects occur when toxins are released from the body. A hot seaweed bath is like a wet-steam sauna, only better, because the kelps and sea greens balance body chemistry instead of dehydrating it. The electrolytic magnetic action of the sea plants releases excess body fluids from congested cells, and dissolves fatty wastes through the skin, replacing them with depleted minerals, especially iodine and potassium. Sea plants alkalize the body with mineral riches easily absorbed through the pores.
KELP, KOMBU, BLADDERWRACK, DULSE, SEA GRASSES.

Why is massage therapy good for depression?

The biggest problem in stress-caused depression is reduced energy or fatigue. Massage therapy deals directly with skeletal-muscular areas where tenseness shows up - the stiff neck, the tight shoulders, the aching back. During massage, constricted muscles get stretched and relaxed. This improves circulation, which increases energy and reduces anxiety.

In addition, massage therapists learn how to have a nurturing touch - long, flowing strokes that can alleviate even severe, clinical depression. In this case, more **is** better - once a week is good, twice a week is excellent if you suffer from chronic anxiety. And regularity is most important, since a tell-tale attribute of serious depression is

that the feeling of well-being can't last. The actual anti-depressant effects of a half hour massage last from 3 to 36 hours, but more importantly, it re-educates the body. People who go on a regular therapeutic massage program report that massage helps their bodies "remember" what it feels like to be comfortable, relaxed and cared for. I, myself have experienced this phenomenon.

How does guided imagery work for stress and depression?

Imagery is simply a flow of thoughts that one can see, hear, feel, smell, or taste in one's imagination. It is a natural way the nervous system stores, accesses, and processes information, making it especially effective for maintaining the dialogue between mind and body. The immune system, brain and other vital body systems communicate, connect with and influence one another. This way of communicating with oneself is a source of power in the healing process that is effective in dealing with almost any medical situation where problem solving, decision making, relaxation, or symptom relief is useful. (On the down side, as many of us know, when the brain allows stress levels to get out of control, it can have a detrimental impact on the immune system.)

Imagery assists "in clarifying attitudes, emotions, behavior and lifestyle patterns that may be involved in producing illness." **Guiding the imagery** is a proven method for pain relief, for helping people tolerate medical procedures, for reducing side effects, and for stimulating healing responses in the body. It can help people find meaning in their illness, offer a way to cope, and accelerate recovery.

We know that learning to relax is fundamental to self-healing, and imagery is a part of almost all relaxation and stress-reduction techniques. For many people, imagery is the easiest way to learn to relax, and its active nature makes it more comfortable than other relaxation methods.

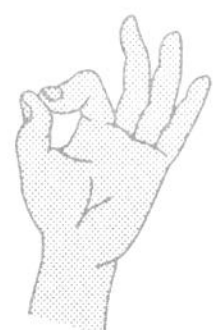

There are two types of guided imagery:

♣Receptive imagery involves entering into a relaxed state, then concentrating on the area of the body that is ailing. The idea is to envision an embodiment of the illness and ask it why it is causing the trouble.

♣Active imagery involves envisioning an illness being cured. This may mean anything from imagining your immune system attacking a tumor to picturing pain as a ball rolling out of your body.

— **The mind and body are inseparable. Everything that is registered in our minds is also registered in our bodies.** —

Messages from the brain through the nervous system are instantaneous. Thoughts also register through the endocrine system, triggering the hypothalmic-pituitary-adrenal axis.

Stress is an excellent example of an emotional response to life's difficult situations that manifests itself in the body. By directly accessing emotions through guided imagery a person can better understand the needs that may be represented by stress and can help develop ways to meet those needs.

A specific example of this would be a person's response to the loss of a spouse with a prolonged state of depression. The body will also be in a prolonged state of depression, making the person susceptible to serious health problems. But if the person is able to intergrate the loss into a broader meaning of life, the loss does not overwhelm, and grief lessens over time. Gradually a more wholesome view of life can be experienced, where the person again becomes a participant in life rather than a victim of its circumstances.

Are you stressed out? The stress stages below can indicate your stress levels.

There seem to be four stages to stress symptoms.

1) losing interest in enjoyable activities, sagging at the corners of the eyes, creasing of the forehead, becoming short-tempered, bored, nervous.
2) fatigue, anger, insomnia, paranoia, sadness.
3) chronic head and neck aches, high blood pressure, upset stomach, older appearance.
4) skin disorders, kidney malfunction, susceptibility to frequent infections, asthma, heart disease, mental breakdown.

Most people under stress also have trouble getting enough sleep and rest - the very thing that can most quickly improve the body's ability to deal with stress. There is a normal daily cycle between "fight or flight" and relaxation. Chronic stress arises when the relaxation phase is missed. Latest studies show that about 15% of the American population - 36 million people, receive sedative drug prescriptions every year for chronic stress symptoms. Most of these prescriptions are highly addictive benzodiazepine compounds, such as Valium (30 million prescriptions), that should be used in conjunction with psychotherapy. The same study shows that almost 50 million people regularly use over-the-counter sedatives and sleeping pills. The abusive/addictive potential of these medications is not as great, but the body builds in a certain immunity to them, so that more and more needs to be taken to get the same effect.

Herbal compounds that relax and help rebuild the nervous system are a better choice for many people; they do not have the serious side effects or addictive potential. Herbs can be as effective as prescription tranquilizer drugs in controlling stress, especially when used before retiring. They are calming, relaxing and fast-working to encourage sweet sleep. Since different nervine herbs act through entirely different pathways in the body, it is more effective to use them in combination than to take them alone.

Three choices for better sleep and relaxation are given below:

- **An extract formula: VALERIAN RT., SCULLCAP LF., HOPS, PASSION FLWR., WILD LETTUCE.**

- A gentle, relaxing tea blend:
CHAMOMILE, SPEARMINT, SCULLCAP, PASSION FLWR., ROSEBUDS, ORANGE BLSM., CATNIP, ROSE HIPS.

- A capsule combination, especially effective for men, who report that it helps them remember their dreams for deeper REM sleep.
VALERIAN RT., SCULLCAP HERB, PASSION FLOWER, KAVA KAVA, HOPS, CARROT CRYSTALS, G.A.B.A. 20MG, TAURINE 20MG, VIT. B6 20MG, NIACIN 10MG.

Stress affects the glands at the deepest levels of the body processes.

The two most stress-involved glands are the adrenals and thyroid.

The adrenals are composed of two parts: the cortex, responsible for cortisone production, and the medulla, which secretes adrenaline. Adrenal cortex helps maintain body balance, regulates carbohydrate and sugar metabolism, dysfunctions that result in diabetes or hypoglycemia and other stress-related diseases. The medulla epinephrine (adrenaline) and norepinaphrine speed up metabolism to cope with stress by warding off its negative effects.

Once again, while the adrenals function to help the body handle stressful situations, chronic stress exhausts them, especially when the normal body relaxation cycle keeps getting missed. (See previous page.) Nourishing stress-depleted adrenal glands is one of the primary actions to take in combatting fatigue and low energy. Herbs can supply nutrients to stimulate and nourish exhausted adrenals so that cortical production and energy can be restored. They offer adrenal support without adding stimulants or raw animal glandular tissue. Two effective examples are given below:

- The first, an extract formula, has proven more useful for men:

LICORICE, BLADDERWRACK, SARSAPARILLA RT., IRISH MOSS.

- The second is a capsule combination, more useful for women:

LICORICE, SARSAPARILLA, BLADDERWRACK, UVA URSI, ROSE HIPS/VIT. C, IRISH MOSS, GINGER, ASTRAGALUS RT., CAPSICUM, PANTOTHENIC ACID 25MG, VIT. B6 20MG, BETAINE HCL.

Thyroid malfunction may be responsible for up to 15% of all depression cases. Synthetic thyroid hormones regularly prescribed may have uneven reactions and side effects. An herbal formula for thyroid health usually relies on sea plants as a gentle, safe source of iodine. The thyroid uses this mineral source to perform its own "balancing act," raising or reducing its output as needed. An effective "iodine therapy" combination might look like this:
KELP, KOMBU, DULSE, ALFALFA, WATERCRESS, BORAGE, IRISH MOSS, SPIRULINA, NETTLES.

STRESS & YOUR HEART

Stress constricts the arterial system, creating greater circulatory disease risk.

The price for years of stress can be high blood pressure, cardiovascular disease, and congestive heart failure, along with myriad other problems. The medical profession estimates that up to 90% of all visits are stress-related.

In our experience, herbal combinations along with important diet and lifestyle improvements can make a major difference to your heart health and your life expectancy.

Did you know that you can carve out health with your own knife and fork? Or that almost all circulatory diseases can be treated and prevented with diet and nutrition improvement? We all know that refined, fatty, high calorie foods create cardiovascular problems, but did you know that a natural foods diet will relieve them? Fried foods, salty foods, sugary foods, low fiber foods, pasteurized dairy products, red meats and processed meats, tobacco, hard liquor and caffeine are all hard on your heart and arteries. A diet that emphasizes fresh, whole fiber foods, high mineral foods with lots of potassium and magnesium, oxygen-rich foods from green vegetables, sprouts and wheat germ (wheat germ oil can raise the oxygen level of the heart as much as 30%), and vegetable proteins will bring high rewards - a longer, healthier life - and control of your life.

Circulatory problems of high blood pressure, irregular heartbeat and congestive heart failure are tied to stress reactions. Herbal formulas can address each of these problems well.

An effective, fast-working combination to reduce high blood pressure tones and stimulates the entire arterial and venous structure. The formula is based on garlic, hawthorne and Siberian ginseng, three well-known, clinically proven heart and circulatory tonics. The herbs are rich in flavonoids to support better vein and capillary integrity, with gentle stimulants to increase circulatory flow. The formula includes mild herbal diuretics to keep the body from retaining fluid. It looks like this:
GARLIC, HAWTHORNE LF., FLWR. & BRY., SIBERIAN GINSENG, DANDELION RT., PARSLEY RT., GINGER, CAPSICUM, HEARTSEASE, GOLDENSEAL RT., BILBERRY LF. & BRY., VIT. B6 15MG.

A formula for congestive heart failure will help clear occlusions, stabilize the heart beat, strengthen arterial structure, reduce excess fluid, and increase anti-oxidant and free radical scavenging activity. The one below is especially effective for cardio-pulmonary conditions where there is shortness of breath. It should be used for one to three months.
HAWTHORN LF. AND FLWR., SIBERIAN GINSENG, GINKGO BILOBA, ASTRAGALUS, COQ10-30MG., PORIA COCOS MUSHROOM, UVA URSI, CITRUS BIOFLAVONOIDS -100MG., VIT. E-30MG.

❦ The combination below is particularly beneficial for women who have entered menopause and feel that they are more at risk for stress-related heart problems. It noticeably invigorates blood circulation throughout the body, tones the heart muscle, guards against fibrillation or palpitations by regulating heartbeat, and helps prevent high blood pressure reactions by keeping the arterial/venous structure toned and elastic. We have heard many reports from women that it gives them an overall feeling of well being.
HAWTHORN LF., FLWR. & BRY., SIBERIAN GINSENG, MOTHERWORT, BILBERRY LF. & BRY., HEARTSEASE LF., CAPSICUM, ASTRAGALUS RT., LECITHIN, GINKGO BILOBA, D-ALPHA VIT. E PWD. 20IU, CHOLINE 15MG, NIACIN 15MG.

❦ **SIBERIAN GINSENG EXTRACT** - as a single herb is a superior adaptogen that increases energy, reduces stress and combats fatigue. It works through the adrenal glands to support their ability to withstand stress. It strengthens the entire circulatory system, and is a specific for reducing high blood pressure.

Stress has an equal, if not more dramatic effect on digestive health than your daily diet.

Your body tells you in a variety of unpleasant ways that you are under stress - all the way from "butterflies" in your stomach to nausea to a full-blown, bleeding ulcer. Don't let it get that far. Let herbs add their powerful enzyme therapy to your tension-fighting arsenal.

✹The following simple, gentle tea has been used for centuries to calm a nervous stomach, sweeten the breath, and end a meal with a feeling of well-being rather than heartburn.
PEPPERMINT, PAPAYA, ROSEMARY, HIBISCUS FLOWERS.

✹If your needs are greater, a pre-meal herbal enzyme like the one below can add nutrients that can help even major digestive upsets

such as those caused by a reaction to drugs. Herbal enzymes also aid digestion through acid/alkaline balance. Eating under stress means that the proper enzymes often don't come into play at the right time for the right food. The herbs in this extract formula combine easily with digestive juices to enhance enzyme activity.
FENNEL SD., GINGER, PAPAYA SD., TURMERIC, PEPPERMINT, SPEARMINT, CRAMP BARK, CATNIP.

✷Licorice root is a specific herb that protects the digestive system from damage caused by stress, and naturally promotes healing of both gastric and duodenal ulcers. Response to its use in clinical tests is outstanding for both chronic duodenal, and acute gastric ulcers. Rather than suppressing acid release into the stomach as most drugs do, an herbal digestive formula containing licorice encourages normal immune defenses that prevent ulcer formation. Licorice help protect a healthy mucosal lining in the intestinal tract, and may be taken as needed to sooth burning and the pain of inflammation. Used over a two to three month period, a licorice ulcer compound would be effective in rebuilding healthy tissue and providing enzyme therapy for better food use.
A capsule formula might look like this:
GOLDENSEAL RT., SLIPPERY ELM, LICORICE, MYRRH, CALENDULA FLWR., CAPSICUM, BILBERRY.

Stress puts the immune system under attack

Adaptogen-based formulas help the body handle stress, renew vitality and relieve fatigue.

At the end of the day, the best way for our bodies to deal with chronic stress is to have strong immune response. Providing ourselves with the best diet possible, and following a few simple watchwords is the best defense against stress.

Some of these checkpoints include:

1. Take a high potency, concentrated, green, "superfood" twice a week. Chlorella, barley grass, spirulina, and alfalfa would all fall into this category. The composition of chlorophyll is very similar to that of human plasma, so these foods provide a "mini-transfusion" for your bloodstream.
2. Include sea vegetables, such as kelp, dulse, kombu, or wakame in your diet for their therapeutic iodine, high potassium, and sodium alginate content.
3. Take a high potency lactobacillus or acidophilus complex, for friendly gastrointestinal flora, and good food assimilation.
4. Include an anti-oxidant supplement, such as vitamin E with selenium, beta carotene, zinc, CoQ 10, pycnogenol or vitamin C to protect against free radical damage, and oxygen deficiency.
Several herbs also have strong anti-oxidant qualities: echinacea, chaparral, goldenseal rt., Siberian ginseng, rosemary, astragalus, suma, burdock, and pau d' arco.
5. Protect the thymus gland from shrinking with age by nourishing this immune organ with a raw thymus glandular supplement.
6. Aerobic exercise keeps circulation flowing and system oxygen high. Disease does not readily overrun a body where oxygen and organic minerals are high in the vital fluids.
7. The immune system is stimulated by a few minutes of early morning sunlight every day. Avoid excessive sun. Sun **burn** depresses immunity.
8. Finally, laugh a lot. Laughter lifts more than your spirits. It also boosts the immune system. Laughter decreases cortisol, an immune suppressor, allowing immune boosters to function better.

Tonic herbs are good immune boosters.

Modern immune studies in the herb world have concentrated on adaptogens - substances that put the body into a state of heightened resistance. As premier adaptogens, we have found ginsengs to be an excellent choice as immune stimulators. Ginsengs from around the world offer the widest range of revitalizing activity.
A defense-restoring tea might look like this:
PRINCE, KIRIN, AMERICAN - ARALIA, BRAZILIAN - SUMA, SIBERIAN - ELEUTHERO, TIENCHI), PAU D'ARCO, ECHINACEA ANGUSTIFOLIA & PURPUREA, REISHI MUSHROOM, ASTRAGALUS RT., ST. JOHN'S WORT, MA HUANG, FENNEL SD.

An immune system stengthening drink might rely on brown rice and miso for its building blocks. The following formula balances the acid/alkaline system, regulates body fluid osmosis and electrical activity in the nervous system, and aids digestion and regularity. It is a rich chlorophyll, green vitamin source, with large amounts of plant beta-carotene, B vitamins, choline, essential fatty acids with GLA, D-GLA and linoleic acid, and octacosonal for tissue oxygen. It is a vigorous source of usable proteins and amino acids, has almost twice the amount of protein as a comparable amount of wheat germ, and of course comes without the fats and density of animal protein. It is an exceptional source of alkalizing enzymes for assimilation and digestion, and for all cell functions.
MISO BROTH PWD., SOY PROTEIN, TAMARI PWD., CRANBERRY JUICE PWD., BREWER'S YEAST, VEGETABLE ACIDOPHILUS, ALFALFA, BORAGE SD, YELLOW DOCK, OATSTRAW, DANDELION LF., BARLEY GRASS PWD., LICORICE, WATERCRESS, PAU D'ARCO, NETTLES, HORSETAIL HERB, RED RASPBERRY LF., FENNEL SD., SEBERIAN GINSENG, PARSLEY RT. & LF., BILBERRY, SCHIZANDRA, ROSEMARY, DULSE, WAKAME, KOMBU, SEA PALM.

The following "feel great" capsule combination is an over-all body tonic to enhance daily rejuvenation and ease stress. It contains a wide range of herbal heavyweights for energy and stamina. It provides usable anti-oxidants for better immune defense, mental clarity, and a feeling of well-being. It helps clean and alkalize the blood, increases circulation, provides absorbable minerals and enzyme precursors. It may be used on a daily basis.
BEE POLLEN, SIBERIAN GINSENG (ELEUTHERO), GOTU KOLA LF., SARSAPARILLA RT., LICORICE, SUMA BK., SCHIZANDRA BRY., SPIRULINA, AMERICAN GINSENG (PANAX), RICE PROTEIN, ALFALFA, WILD CHERRY BK., BLACK COHOSH, KELP, GOLDENSEAL RT., HAWTHORNE LF., FLWR. & BRY., BARLEY GRASS, NUTRITIONAL YEAST, GINKGO BILOBA LF., CAPSICUM, CHOLINE 10MG, ZINC (GLUCONATE) 3MG.

About Tension Headaches

We know that most headaches are stress-related. What natural treatments are most effective for tension headaches?

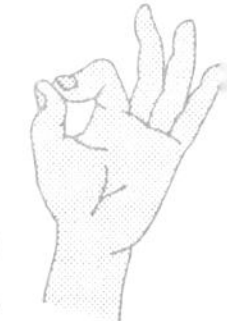

Tension headaches are chronic for most people under stress. It is the most common complaint we hear. The good news is that herbal analgesics **are** effective for these headaches. In general, tension headaches stem from the pain center at the base of the brain. Herbal analgesics can address very specific body areas, so they are a good choice for the types of stress headaches pain originating in this region. They work by soothing membranes, relaxing muscles and spasms, calming the mind, and providing oxygen or warmth for relief. They allow you to think clearly, and carry on with your life, while you work on stress-reducing techniques that will address the cause of the problem. All of them allow your body full function and communication with you while it is healing.

Chemical painkilling drugs, though strong, afford relief by masking pain, or deadening certain body mechanisms so that they cannot function. Herbal pain relievers are more subtle and work at a deeper level - to relax, soothe, ease and calm the distressed area. Natural pain relievers allow you to use pain for information about your body, yet not be overwhelmed by the trauma to body and spirit that unrelieved suffering can bring.

The formulas on this page are specifically targeted to stress headaches. Pick one for your symptoms.

❁ This stress relief extract is calming, soothing, restorative, **and strong**. It is especially helpful in relieving nerve pain and muscle constriction. Improvement is often felt within 20 minutes.
BLACK COHOSH RT., SCULLCAP LF., BLACK HAW, WOOD BETONY, KAVA KAVA, CARROT EXT., HONEY.

❁ This therapeutic blend is for those who like the tissue relaxing warmth of a hot tea. It soothes body aches, calms nerves and relieves stress headaches.
CATNIP, ROSEMARY, CHAMOMILE, PEPPERMINT, BLUE VIOLET, WOOD BETONY, GOTU KOLA, FEVERFEW FLWR., WHITE WILLOW BARK, BLESSED THISTLE.

❁ These capsules act as a relaxant and vaso-dilator for neural pain in the neck and base of the brain. They encourage body balance by providing nerve and brain nutrients. They often work when nothing else has been successful.
WILD LETTUCE, FEVERFEW, VALERIAN, ROSEMARY, LICORICE, CATNIP, EURO. MISTLETOE, GENTIAN RT., DL-PHENYL.- 15MG.

❁ These capsules are a strong, targeted combination to address the causes of cluster headaches and certain types of chronic mi-

graines. When taken on a regular basis they may used as both a control and preventive for this type of headache.
FEVERFEW FLWR., VALERIAN RT., WILD LETTUCE, CULTIVATED LADY SLIPPER RT., GINKGO BILOBA, GOLDENSEAL RT., NIACIN 15MG.

This tea is for people who suffer from frequent cluster headaches. It is particularly helpful against this type of headache when taken as a hot drink. It may be used both symptomatically and as a body balancer toward prevention. It is particularly effective if taken before a cranial or spinal adjustment by a chiropractor or massage therapist.
FEVERFEW, WILD LETTUCE, VALERIAN, LADY SLIPPER, GINKGO BILOBA, NIACINAMIDE 60MG.

Can the scientific art of aromatherapy help relieve stress headaches?

Healers all over the world have become newly facinated with the ancient science of aromatherapy, a centuries-old art that uses pure essential oils or aromatic extracts form certain plants to promote physical, mental and emotional health, and to restore body balance and harmony. Aromatherapists have known for thousands of years that volatile aromas of essential oils directly affect the brain, some producing calming effects, and others mental stimulation. Europe is on the forefront of the aromatherapy renaissance, where currently several thousand medical practitioners prescribe essential oils for a variety of ailments.

Aromatherapy's essential oils effect different people in different ways and on different levels. Aroma itself is only one of the active healing qualities. The oils exert much of their therapeutic effect through their pharmacological properties and their small molecular size, making them one of the few medicinal agents easily absorbed by the body. The benefits of essential oils can be obtained through inhalation, external application or ingestion.
When inhaled, the odors stimulate a release of neurotransmitters, chemicals responsible for pleasant feelings and pain reduction.
Applied topically, essential oils' molecules penetrate the pores below the surface of the skin. The molecules course through the fluids between cells and find their way into the bloodstream and from there, throughout the body.

The immediate and profound effect that essential oils have on the central nervous system makes aromatherapy an excellent method for stress management.

The aroma of **apples and cinnamon** has a powerful stabilizing effect on some people, especially those suffering from nervous anxiety. This aroma alone is capable of lowering blood pressure and preventing panic attacks.

Chamomile and lavender exert a calm and relaxing effect.

Rosemary is a powerful central nervous system stimulant.

Peppermint eases headaches.

Pine oil is used to balance breathing and refreshthe body.

Cassia is exotic, seductive, warming and relaxing.

Coriander warms, relaxes, deodorizes and soothes.

Clary sage calms edgy nerves.

Neroli is a stress reducer, and has sedative and deep relaxant properties.

Orange, jasmine and rose have a tranquilizing effect and work by altering the brain waves into a rhythm that produces calmness and a sense of well-being.

Mandarin is calming and a key choice for helping to release anxiety.

Roman Chamomile calms an upset mind or body. A drop rubbed on the solar plexus can bring rapid relief of mental or physical stress.

Stress & Addictions Go Hand In Hand

Drug abuse in one form or another has become a fact of modern life. American's high stress lifestyles deplete energy reserves, motivating quick "high voltage fixes" to overcome fatigue and relieve tension or boredom. Using drugs, sugar, alcohol, nicotine or caffeine as body fuel creates multiple deficiencies of vitamins, minerals, essential fatty acids, amino acids and enzymes. This depletion sets off a chain reaction which results in stress and craving for nutrients. The process keeps repeating in a futile effort to satisfy increasing need, and addiction eventually occurs.

For most people, this is just the beginning. Drug-caused malnutrition and reduced immunity swiftly lead to hypothyroidism, chronic fatigue syndrome, and auto-immune diseases such as mononucleosis, hepatitis, M.S. and AIDS- related syndromes. Even if these serious disorders are avoided, consequences of drug use are high. Drug abusers and potential drug abusers are always either sick or coming down with something. As soon as one cold, sore throat, bout of "flu," or bladder infection is treated, a new one takes its place. Work is impaired, job time is lost, and family and social life is greatly affected.

Concentrated nutritional support is an essential key to recovery from addictions. The overwhelming majority of habitual addictive substance users suffer from nutrient deficiencies and metabolic or nutritional imbalances. When these conditions are corrected, the need to get high by artificial means is sharply diminished. Herbs can establish a solid foundation for rebuilding a depleted system. Give yourself plenty of time for regeneration. It often takes up to a year to detoxify and clear drugs from the bloodstream.

Herbs can help overcome addictions.

A three stage program brings the most positive results:

1) CLEANSE the body of drug residues from your body as quickly as you can. Get a cleansing massage from a good massage therapist to help normalize your system. Take a hot sauna two or three times a week; or the sweating herbal bath below:

JABORANDI, PENNYROYAL, ORANGE PEEL AND BLOSSOMS, THYME, ANGELICA RT. ELDER FLOWERS, KESU FLOWERS.

- Clean your lymph system with **ECHINACEA EXTRACT** drops.
- Clean your liver with the following liver flush tea:

DANDELION RT., WATERCRESS, YELLOW DOCK, PAU D'ARCO, HYSSOP, PARSLEY LF., OREGON GRAPE RT., RED SAGE, LICORICE, MILK THISTLE SD., HIBISCUS FLWR.

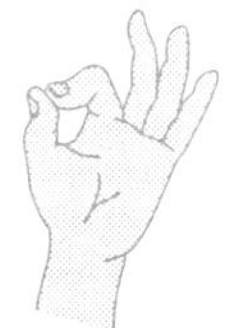

2) STRENGTHEN your nervous system and adrenals with herbal formulas like the ones below:

For the adrenals, a combination to increase energy without adding stimulants.
LICORICE, SARSAPARILLA, BLADDERWRACK, UVA URSI, ROSE HIPS/VIT. C, IRISH MOSS, GINGER, ASTRAGALUS RT., CAPSICUM, PANTOTHENIC ACID 25MG, VIT. B6 20MG, BETAINE HCL.

For the nerves, a complex broad spectrum herbal nervine to help control many of the problems faced during withdrawal from drugs or alcohol. This formula is a positive factor in "getting over the hump." It is designed to depress craving, overcome nervous tension and low energy, help rebuild damaged nerve structure, encourage restful sleep, soothe withdrawal headaches, and increase attention span and focus.
SCULLCAP HERB, SIBERIAN GINSENG, KAVA KAVA, ASCORBATE VIT. C 70MG, VALERIAN RT., ALFALFA EXT. PWD., WOOD BETONY, DLPA 35MG., NIACIN 35MG, LICORICE, CAPSICUM.

3) BALANCE your system with adaptogen/hormone balancing herbs such as the restorative formula below:
GINSENGS (PRINCE, KIRIN, AMERICAN - ARALIA, BRAZILIAN - SUMA, SIBERIAN - ELEUTHERO, TIENCHI), PAU D'ARCO, ECHINACEA ANGUSTIFOLIA & PURPUREA, REISHI MUSHROOM, ASTRAGALUS RT., ST. JOHN'S WORT, MA HUANG, FENNEL SD.

Most people recovering from addictions find their energy levels are very low as the body tries to carry on without its usual "high voltage fix". Herbs can help you through the energy crunch. The following high energy tea encourages better use of the body's own energy supply, and is an excellent "weaning" tea for withdrawal fatigue. It may be made up and sipped throughout the day.
GOTU KOLA, AMERICAN GINSENG ROOT FIBER, PRINCE GINSENG, DAMIANA, KAVA KAVA, RED CLOVER, RASPBERRY, PEPPERMINT, CLOVES.

Don't forget regular exercise and deep breathing during this period. These things will help keep your mind clear, your head on straight, and your body cleansed of toxins.

Work Addiction Is Becomng The Stress Hazard Of The Nineties

A major fallout of America's deficit spending eighties was that more than one member of a family had to work to keep the family at the same standard of living. If a family or individual wanted to **raise** their standard of living, they had to take on another job or extra work projects. Nineties families often have both husband and wife working two jobs, and teenage children working one or more jobs, too. It's easy to see how a workaholic lifstyle came into being and how work addiction insinuated itself into our society. Work addicts have been described as living in misery amid applause, slaps on the back, fat paychecks and performance awards.

Ten signs of work addiction include:

1) A total lack of balance between work and other areas of life. Work addicts don't feel like they are worth much unless they are working. And regardless of how much they actually work, they tell themselves and everybody else that it is much more.

2) The inability to admit limitations for themselves. Consequently, they drive themselves, (and often their work associates) beyond human endurance. In addition, because of overcommitting, they hardly ever think a project through before jumping into it, or finish the project on time.

3) They judge themselves against unrealistic standards - and usually feel that nobody can do a job as well as they can. They delegate little, piling more on themselves under the guise of quality control.

4) They find it very hard to relax or have fun, feeling anxious and worthless when they aren't working. Any activity that isn't "productive" is a complete waste of time to them. They have trouble letting go of work even when they aren't physically working, and tend to tune out everything else while they plan and think about work. A bizarre side effect of this that is that work addicts suffer "brown out amnesia" about things they did or conversations they had that weren't about work.

5) Most work addicts had strict, serious, puritanical upbringing. Consequently, they take themselves and their work very seriously with very little humor or acceptance of human frailties. The

opposite side to this fact is that they are very responsible when it comes to getting a job of work done, but not very responsible at all about family commitments

6) They have a hard time with personal relationships - not only because they always have their minds on work, but because they set standards of perfection for loved ones that are impossible to meet. Work is used as shield that helps them avoid conflicts with their inner selves and their loved ones.

7) Time is the most precious commodity for a work addict. They cannot tolerate waiting, whether it be for an appointment, behind a slower car in front of them, or in a movie line. They are constantly racing against the clock. The down side is that they get there faster but lose all attention to details.

8) Work addiction is usually adrenaline addiction. So work addicts tend to turn every situation into crisis management to turn on the adrenaline high.

9) They have an enormous sense of urgency and need immediate gratification for their efforts. Most work addicts are so over-extended that their attention span is almost nil. They will rush a job through so that they can chalk up another notch on their accomplishments. The product is far more important to them than the process.

10) They are so wedded to their work that they lose the ability to make good judgements about it - work conditions, fairness, salary, advancement. Often, they become victims of the very process that they devote their lives to.

Getting unstuck from addiction to work

- Try some relaxating, stress-reducing techniques, such as yoga, meditation, daily walks, etc. The following relaxing, restoring herbal compound can help, too.

BLACK HAW, BLACK COHOSH, HOPS, CULTIVATED LADY SLIP-PER, SCULLCAP, KAVA KAVA, VALERIAN RT., WOOD BETONY, EUROPEAN MISTLETOE, LOBELIA, OATSTRAW.

- Strengthen family ties. At the end of the day, family is what counts most. Its easy to start by celebrating a family event, tradition, or anniversary.

- Make a conscious effort to slow down. Stop and smell a rose or two. Learn to say no when you already have too much on your plate.

- Rekindle friendships you have let go because of work. Make some new friends. Friends are godsends of support. Caring about each other expands your interests outside of work.

- Develop a hobby or creative outlet that you've always wanted to try.

- Improve your diet and get more rest. Live one day at a time.

A Last Word About Herbs

Science can only quantify, isolate, and assay to understand. Herbs respond to these methods, but they are so much more than a scientific breakdown. God shows his face a little in herbs. Like mankind, herbs also have an ineffable quality. Fortunately for mankind, our bodies know how to use herbs without our brains having to know why.

Albath, W. "Anti-Inflammatory Substances in Chamomile Oil." **Archives of Experimental Pathology and Pharmacology.** 193 (1939): 619-21.

Banerjee, B.X., and J.A. Izquierdo. "Antistress and Antifatigue Properties of Panax Ginseng: Comparison with Piracetam." **Acta Physiol. Lat. Am.** 32(4) (1982): 277-85.

Bauer, R., et al. "Immunological In Vivo Examinations of Echinacea Extracts." Arzneim-Forsch. 38 (2) 1988: 276-81.

Brekhman, I.I., and I.V. Dardymov. "New Substances of Plant Origin Which Increase Non-Specific Resistance." **Ann. Rev. Pharmacol.** 9 (1969): 419-30.

Brown, Donald J., N.D. Update on Adaptogenic Medicine: FAIM Education Fund Seminar. New York: June 20, 1992.

Foster, Steven. **Chamomile.** Austin: American Botanical Council. 1990.

---. **Echinacea: Nature's Immune Enhancer.** Rochester: Healing Arts Press, 1991.

---. **Valerian.** Austin: American Botanical Council, 1990.

Hobbs, Christopher. **Foundations of Health: The Liver & Digestive Herbal.** Capitola: Botanica Press, 1992.

Houghton, P.J. "The Biological Activity of Valerian and Related Plants." **Journal of Ethnopharmacology.** 22 (1988): 121-42.

Kim, C., et al. "Influence of Ginseng on the Stress Mechanism." **Lloydia.** 33 (1970): 43-48.

Leatherwood, P.D., et al. "Aqueous Extract of Valerian Root (Valeriana Officinalis) Improves Sleep Quality in Man." **Pharmacology, Biochemistry and Behavior.** 17 (1982): 65-71.

Mowrey, Daniel B., Ph.D. **Next Generation Herbal Medicine.** New Canaan: Keats Publishing, 1990.

Shahani, Khem M., and Custy F. Fernandez. "Anticarcinogenic and Immunological Properties of Dietary Lactobacilli." University of Nebraska, Lincoln. Sept. 11, 1989.

Teeguarden, Ron. **Chinese Tonic Herbs.** New York: Japan Publications, Inc., 1985.

Wagner, H., et al. "Drugs with Adaptogenic Effects for Strengthening the Powers of Resistance." **Zeitschrift fur Phytotherapie.** 13 (1992): 42-54

Weiss, Rudolf Fritz, M.D. **Herbal Medicine.** Beaconsfield: Beaconsfield Publishing, 1988.

Zhang, Y., et al. "The Anti-Leukocytopenic and Anti-Stress Effects of Astragalus Saponins on Mice." **Nanjing Yixueyuan Xuebao.** 12 (1992): 244-8.

Dr. Page's written papers are thoroughly researched - through empirical observation as well as from internationally documented evidence. Studies are ongoing and updated. If you desire reference material, send a self-addressed, stamped envelope with your request to Healthy Healing Publications, 16060 Via Este, Sonora, Ca., 95370.

ABOUT THE AUTHOR

Linda Rector-Page has been working in the fields of nutrition and herbal medicine both professionally and as a personal lifestyle choice, since the early seventies. She is a certified Doctor of Naturopathy and Ph.D., with extensive experience in formulating and testing herbal combinations. She received a Doctorate of Naturopathy from the Clayton School of Holistic Healing in 1988, and a Ph.D. in Nutritional Therapy from the American Holistic College of Nutrition in 1989. She is a member of both the American and California Naturopathic Medical Associations.

Linda opened and operated the "Rainbow Kitchen", a natural foods restaurant, then became a working partner in The Country Store Natural Foods store. She has written four successful books and a library series of booklets in the nutritional healing field. She is the founder/developer of Crystal Star Herbal Nutrition.

Broad, continuous research in all aspects of the alternative healing world, from manufacturers, to stores to consumers has been the cornerstone of success for her reference work **"HEALTHY HEALING"**, now in its ninth edition. Crystal Star Herbal Nutrition products, which are formulated by Linda, are carried by over twenty-five hundred natural food stores nationwide. Feedback from these consumer sources provides up-to-the-minute contact with the needs and results experienced by people taking more responsibility for their own health. Much of the lifestyle information and empirical observation in her books comes from this direct experience - knowledge that is then translated into Crystal Star Herbal Nutrition products, and recorded in every **"HEALTHY HEALING"** edition.

"COOKING FOR HEALTHY HEALING," now in its second new edition, is a companion to **"HEALTHY HEALING".** It draws on both the recipes from the Rainbow Kitchen and the defined, lifestyle diets that she has developed from healing results since then. The book contains 33 separate diet programs, and over 900 healthy recipes. Every recipe has been taste-tested and time-tested as part of each recommended diet so that the healing suggestions can be easily maintained with optimum nutrition.

In **"HOW TO BE YOUR OWN HERBAL PHARMACIST",** Linda addresses the rising appeal of herbs and herbal healing in America. Many people are taking an interest in clearly understanding herbal formulation knowledge for personal use. This book is designed for those wishing to take more definitive responsibility for their health through individually developed herbal combinations.

Linda's newest work is a party reference book called **"PARTY LIGHTS"** in collaboration with restaurateur Doug Vanderberg. **"PARTY LIGHTS"** takes healthy cooking one step further by adding in the fun to a good diet. Over sixty party themes are completely planned in this new book, all with healthy party foods, earthwise decorations, professional garnishing tips, festive napkin folding, interesting games and activities.

Published by Healthy Healing Publications, 1995.